J 599.76 JOB

Jobes, Cecily

Watch out for skunks!

S   5/16

WILD BACKYARD ANIMALS

Watch Out for

SKUNKS!

Cecily Jobes

PowerKiDS press.

New York

Published in 2016 by The Rosen Publishing Group, Inc.
29 East 21st Street, New York, NY 10010

First Edition

Editor: Caitlin McAneney
Book Design: Katelyn Heinle/Tanya Dellaccio

Photo Credits: Cover, p. 11 Heiko Kiera/Shutterstock.com; p. 4 The Len/Shutterstock.com; p. 5 Adwo/Shutterstock.com; p. 6 Volodymyr Burdiak/Shutterstock.com; p. 7 (Spotted Skunk) Rick & Nora Bowers/Visuals Unlimited, Inc./Getty Images; p. 7, 9 (striped skunk) Critterbiz/Shutterstock.com; p. 7 (hog-nosed skunk) Agustin Esmoris/Shutterstock.com; p. 8 Big Pants Production/Shutterstock.com; p. 13 Joe McDonald/Getty Images; p. 15 Holly Kuchera/Shutterstock.com; p. 17 135pixels/Shutterstock.com; p. 19 Bildagentur Zoonar GmbH/Shutterstock.com; p. 20 Adwo/Shutterstock.com; p. 21 John E Heintz Jr/Shutterstock.com; p. 22 Debbie Steinhausser/Shutterstock.com.

Library of Congress Cataloging-in-Publication Data

Names: Jobes, Cecily.
Title: Watch out for skunks! / Cecily Jobes.
Description: New York : PowerKids Press, 2016. | Series: Wild backyard
  animals | Includes index.
Identifiers: LCCN 2015032215| ISBN 9781508142676 (pbk.) | ISBN 9781508142683
  (6 pack) | ISBN 9781508142690 (library bound)
Subjects: LCSH: Skunks–Juvenile literature.
Classification: LCC QL737.C248 J63 2016 | DDC 599.76/8–dc23
LC record available at http://lccn.loc.gov/2015032215

Manufactured in the United States of America

CPSIA Compliance Information: Batch #BW16PK: For Further Information contact Rosen Publishing, New York, New York at 1-800-237-9932

CONTENTS

WHAT'S THAT SMELL?

You're sitting in your backyard at night, watching the stars. Suddenly, you have to hold your nose. What's that terrible stink?

Skunks are usually to blame for **pungent** nighttime smells. The smell happens when skunks spray predators that get too close. You can smell their spray up to a mile (1.6 km) away! The smell will stick to the skunk's enemy for weeks. Read on to learn more about the stinky skunk!

BACKYARD BITES

If you keep chickens in your backyard, watch out for the sneaky skunk. Skunks like to steal eggs!

YOU MIGHT GUESS A SKUNK HAS BEEN AROUND IF YOU SEE HOLES IN YOUR LAWN, SKUNK TRACKS, OR TORN-UP TRASH CANS.

SKUNKS AT HOME

Where might you find a skunk? These **mammals** are common throughout North America. They're found in most parts of the United States and the more **temperate** areas of Canada. You can also find them in northern Mexico.

Skunks aren't picky about where they make their home. They go where the food is. They live in woods, deserts, and grasslands. They'll make their way into neighborhoods and even cities! That can mean trouble when people and skunks cross paths.

BACKYARD BITES

Not long ago, the Asian stink badger became considered part of the skunk family.

THERE ARE A FEW SPECIES, OR KINDS, OF SKUNKS, BUT STRIPED SKUNKS ARE THE MOST COMMON. WE'LL FOCUS ON STRIPED SKUNKS IN THIS BOOK. OTHER SPECIES INCLUDE THE SPOTTED SKUNK, HOODED SKUNK, AND HOG-NOSED SKUNK.

CANADA

UNITED STATES

MEXICO

SKUNK TERRITORY

STRIPED SKUNK

SPOTTED SKUNK

HOG-NOSED SKUNK

IDENTIFYING A SKUNK

Is that a skunk in your backyard? Skunks are easy to **identify**. They have black and white fur and a bushy tail. Striped skunks have stripes of white down their back. They have long claws that help them dig in the ground for a tasty meal.

Skunks are about the size of a house cat. They grow to around 35 inches (89 cm) long including the tail. Many are smaller than that. Even a heavy skunk weighs only 14 pounds (6.4 kg).

BACKYARD BITES

Skunks have great senses of hearing and smell. That makes up for their poor eyesight.

THESE SKUNKS MAY LOOK FLUFFY AND CUTE, BUT STAY AWAY! THEY CAN EASILY SPRAY YOU.

A STINKY DEFENSE

Larger animals sometimes hunt skunks, but most animals leave them alone. That's because they have a **defense** that keeps predators away.

If a skunk feels unsafe, it will start pounding the ground with its front legs. It might lift its tail, raise its back, and let out a deep growl. That's a warning! If an animal keeps coming closer, the skunk will lift its tail. It sprays a smelly liquid called musk from **glands** at the base of its tail.

SKUNKS LIKE TO AIM FOR THEIR ENEMY'S EYES. THAT WAY, THE ENEMY CAN'T SEE, AND THE SKUNK CAN GET AWAY!

BACKYARD BITES

Skunks often attack when they feel cornered by dogs, cats, people, and other animals. They'll also attack to keep their young safe.

SKUNKS ON THE HUNT

You may never see a skunk hunting unless you're on a night walk. That's because they're nocturnal, or more active at night. Skunks like to eat whatever fruit and plants they can find. They also hunt for bugs and small animals to eat. Eating both plants and animals makes skunks omnivores.

Skunks dig for worms and larvae, or baby bugs. They also eat other bugs, as well as **reptiles**, birds, and fish. Small mammals, such as mice, are another tasty treat.

SKUNKS WILL STEAL BIRD EGGS FROM THEIR NEST IF IT'S LOW ENOUGH TO THE GROUND.

BACKYARD BITES

Like another backyard bandit, the raccoon, skunks will dig through your trash if you leave it outside.

13

A SKUNK'S LIFE

For most of the year, skunks live and hunt alone. That makes them solitary animals. However, in the winter, skunks tend to gather in dens to keep warm. Skunk dens are usually hollow trees or logs, **burrows** left behind by other animals, and buildings left behind by people.

Each year, a mother skunk gives birth to a litter of two to 10 babies. They're called kits. Skunks can spray musk before they even open their eyes!

A MOTHER SKUNK DEFENDS HER KITS FROM PREDATORS. SHE'S NOT AFRAID TO SPRAY HER ENEMIES TO KEEP THEM AWAY!

BACKYARD BITES

Skunks only live around three years in the wild. They live up to 10 years in captivity.

SKUNKS CAUSING TROUBLE

Most of the time, skunks mind their own business. However, if you ever cross paths with one, there could be trouble. If you get too close, a skunk will surely spray you.

More often, dogs have run-ins with these stinky critters. Skunks can spray up to 10 feet (3 m) away. Spray from a skunk can make your pet sick and hurt its eyes. It will also make your pet smell for days. The smell gets even worse if you try to wash your pet in water.

BACKYARD BITES

If a skunk sprays your pet, you can bathe it with a special product you can buy at the store. You can also look up homemade mixes that call for combining dish soap, baking soda, and a **chemical** called hydrogen peroxide.

IT'S IMPORTANT TO TAKE YOUR DOG TO THE VET IF IT SWALLOWED MUSK OR GOT MUSK IN ITS EYES.

Skunks aren't only **dangerous** because of their spray, though. While most mammals are able to carry the rabies virus, the skunk is one of the major carriers. A virus is a small living thing that causes an illness. The rabies virus causes swelling in the brain of animals and people. It almost always leads to death if not treated immediately.

Rabies can be passed by touching brain matter or the spit of an **infected** animal. However, most cases start with a bite by a rabid animal.

ANIMALS WITH RABIES MAY BECOME UNAFRAID OF PEOPLE OR EVEN AGGRESSIVE. OVER TIME, THEY BECOME PARALYZED, OR UNABLE TO MOVE, AND THEY DIE.

BACKYARD BITES

Skunks make up around 25 percent of rabies-positive animals in the United States. In Canada, they make up around 27 percent.

STAYING SAFE WITH SKUNKS

Skunks don't want to harm you. However, if they feel **threatened**, they'll definitely spray you or your pet.

To stay safe, always keep your distance from a skunk. Stay at least 10 feet (3 m) away. To keep your pets safe, don't let them out in the yard at sunrise, sunset, or nighttime. You can also keep food and trash out of your backyard so skunks don't come along in the first place.

SKUNKS ARE HAPPIEST WHEN THEY CAN LIVE AND HUNT IN PEACE.

BACKYARD BITES

Keep an eye on your pets if you let them in your backyard, especially if you smell skunk musk outside.

GOOD NEIGHBORS

Skunks aren't the worst neighbors you can have. In fact, they eat many small animals, which keeps critter populations under control. Skunk populations are doing well, and we don't have to worry about them dying out.

However, it's very important to know how to stay safe around skunks and also how you can keep skunks safe. They may not smell nice, but that doesn't mean you can't be friends from a distance.

GLOSSARY

aggressive: Showing a readiness to attack.

burrow: A hole an animal digs in the ground for shelter.

chemical: Matter that can be mixed with other matter to cause changes.

dangerous: Unsafe.

defense: A way of guarding against an enemy.

gland: A body part that produces something that helps with a bodily function.

identify: To tell what something is.

infected: Having an illness.

mammal: A warm-blooded animal that has a backbone and hair, breathes air, and feeds milk to its young.

pungent: Having a strong, sharp taste or smell.

reptile: A cold-blooded animal with thin, dry pieces of skin called scales.

temperate: Not too hot or too cold.

threatened: Likely to be harmed.

INDEX

WEBSITES

Due to the changing nature of Internet links, PowerKids Press has developed an online list of websites related to the subject of this book. This site is updated regularly. Please use this link to access the list: www.powerkidslinks.com/wba/skunk